TWO PAPERS:

THE GRID

and

CAESURA

TWO PAPERS:
THE GRID
and
CAESURA

Wilfred R. Bion

Karnac Books
London 1989

First published 1977 by Imago Editora Ltda, Rio de Janeiro

This edition published in 1989 by
H. Karnac (Books) Ltd.
58 Gloucester Road
London SW7 4QY

by arrangement with Francesca Bion and Mark Paterson

British Library Cataloguing in Publication Data

Bion, Wilfred R. (Wilfred Ruprecht), *1897–1979*
Two papers: the grid and caesura. – Rev. & Corr. ed.
1. Psychoanalysis
I. Title
150.19'5

ISBN 0–946439–77–X

Printed in Great Britain by BPCC Wheatons Ltd, Exeter

These papers express the core of talks given at meetings of the Los Angeles Psycho-analytic Society in April 1971 (*The Grid*) and June 1975 (*Caesura*).

CONTENTS

TWO PAPERS:

THE GRID

and

CAESURA

THE GRID

THE GRID

	Definitory Hypotheses **1**	ψ **2**	Notation **3**	Attention **4**	Inquiry **5**	Action **6**	**. . . n**
A β-elements	A1	A2				A6	
B α-elements	B1	B2	B3	B4	B5	B6	. . . Bn
C Dream Thoughts Dreams, Myths	C1	C2	C3	C4	C5	C6	. . . Cn
D Pre-conception	D1	D2	D3	D4	D5	D6	. . . Dn
E Conception	E1	E2	E3	E4	E5	E6	. . . En
F Concept	F1	F2	F3	F4	F5	F6	. . . Fn
G Scientific Deductive System		G2					
H Algebraic Calculus							

The Grid is an instrument for the use of practising psycho-analysts. It is not intended that it should be used during the working session.

The left-hand vertical column is an indication of categories in which a statement, of whatever kind, should be placed; this category indicates developmental status.

The horizontal axis is intended to state, approximately, the use to which the statement is being put. The two axes should thus together indicate a category implying a comprehensive range of information about the statement. It has been considered useful to include two rows for β- and α-elements neither of which are real or observable. The β-element row is for the categorization of elements like an unpremeditated blow which is related to, but is not, thought. The next row, C, is intended for categories of thought which are often expressible in terms of sensuous, usually visual, images such as those appearing in dreams, myths, narratives, hallucinations. This category will certainly require extension as psycho-analytic experience accumulates; even now it deserves a 'grid' of its own to expand it suitably for psycho-analytic use.

The use of the remaining categories may become clearer as the paper progresses but it may be as well to anticipate comment on rows G and H. These rows can hardly be said to have any approximation in reality. G is supposed to await the development of psycho-analytic deductive systems, and H the equivalent of algebraic systems. It is to be hoped, as always, that they will not be prematurely developed, for premature development can become as tiresome an obstacle to progress as post-maturity—blindness to what might already be seen to be available for practising or theoretical psycho-analysts.

Row F is intended to represent a category for statements, formulations which already exist. In it can be placed psycho-analytical theories, scientific but non-analytical theories, so called laws of nature and other constructs already accepted by various disciplines as being at least temporarily acceptable as genuine attempts to formulate scientific observations.

The horizontal axis is supposed to fulfil the same scheme with regard to the 'use'. The first column is for definitory hypotheses, however primitive, however sophisticated—as expressed by the row in which it is thought fit to place it or them. About these it may be worth observing that they always presuppose a negative element, that is to say, if I say this paper is about the Grid *that* is what it is about, *not* cookery or measurement etc. Equally, however erroneous my claim may be, however obvious it is to someone else that it *is* about measurement (or cookery or anything else) their formulation is not relevant to this discussion, or any discussion for which the definition has been formulated by the protagonist. Its falsity or otherwise is a function of its relationship to other elements in the scheme. Thus, if, 'we shall leave at sunrise', is stating a definitory hypothesis about the hour of 'our' departure, it is incontrovertible and the fact that an astronomer would consider it to be astronomically incorrect, or a theologian that it is a statement betraying 'hubris', does not controvert the definitory hypothesis. This is my definition of a definitory hypothesis, and as a definition it is a dictate not subject to alteration. The rest of the paper and the various ways in which its elements can be categorized can, however, be criticized as incompatible with the definitory hypothesis.

Column 2 resembles row C in that it requires expansion into a 'grid' of its own. My original idea was that it would supply a series of categories for palpably false statements, preferably known both to the analysand and the analyst to be false, but it was soon evident that it would be necessary to consider what the lie was to be used for, and it was evident at once that 'lie' was a question-begging and possibly misleading term. I remember Melanie Klein saying in the course of a private conversation (and it was a view she expressed more than once) that liars were impossible to treat. I could see that it is a terrible handicap for a psycho-analyst, who depends on being correctly informed, to be habitually and consistently incorrectly informed. I suggested, however, that it could possibly be a form of deep disturbance which was betraying its presence by that form of operation—indeed her theory of projective identification could itself be presented in the course of analysis as a series of lying statements. It became evident that a distinction would need to be made between a lying statement and a false statement, the false statement being related more to the inadequacy of the human being, analyst or analysand alike, who cannot feel confident in his ability to be aware of the 'truth', and the liar who has to be certain of his knowledge of the truth in order to be sure that he will not blunder into it by accident. In short, it was evident that once again the 'use' to which a statement was being put is an essential feature of the practising psycho-analyst's appreciation of his evidence as it unfolds before him. To leave the problem for the time being, it is simplest to consider column 2 as relating to elements known to the analysand to be false, but enshrining statements valuable against the inception of any development in his personality involving catastrophic change. At this unsatisfactory point the discussion must, for the present, be left.

The columns 3, 4, 5 are relatively simple; column 3 approximates to Freud's idea of memory and notation as he describes it in his paper on Two Principles of Mental Functioning. Column 4 comes closer to attention—free floating—with column 5 as more directed to some particular object. The psycho-analyst who is devoting his attention to arranging his schedule has his attention directed to a particular; a patient dominated by feelings of suspicion will likewise be devoting his attention to particular persons or things. Columns 3, 4, and 5 may be conveniently regarded as a spectrum of attention ranging from memory and desire to floating, general attention to a further extreme of particularity. A good example would be the experience of the psycho-analyst when he attends to material seeming to support a theory such as the Oedipal, or the patient seeking to refute or confirm a suspicion that he is admired.

Column 6 is intended to categorize thoughts which are closely related to, or are transformations into, action. This category, like row C and column 2, is one which soon illustrates the difficulties inherent in trying to evolve an instrument which might assist a psycho-analyst to clarify his thinking about his psycho-analytic problems. I wished to find some category in which I could place acting out. At first it seemed helpful but it took very little time to demonstrate its defects. Indeed, I can say that an early casualty in trying to use the Grid is the Grid itself. Nevertheless, its use has made it easier for me to preserve a critical and yet informative, illuminating, attitude to my work. In this respect it has, as far as I am concerned, served a useful purpose which has made me think that others might find it profitable to invent and apply a grid system of their own; in time someone may evolve a more generally acceptable system and proceed from that to the formation of grids suitable for particular types of difficulty, different disciplines and perhaps different nationalities.

The first difficulty to be cleared up is what relationship column 6 bears to row A (β-elements). The intention is to include a category which is not thought at all. Just as it can be argued that Descartes himself in his concept of philosophical doubt failed to doubt the necessity of a thinker—an omission which I have been convinced should be repaired by psycho-analysts—so I think psycho-analysts should entertain the reciprocal belief in personality without thought. In the practice of psycho-analysis it is well known to everyone that patients will often say they 'have no thoughts', or are 'thinking of nothing'. It seems to me that the usual supposition that resistances or denials are operating are theories which have so often proved their value that it would be dangerous, to say the least, to suppose anything else without convincing evidence. Yet I am certain that the psycho-analyst should at least be open to conviction. The existence of a β-element row appears to leave room for such convictions if it should prove useful to entertain them. The column 6 category is intended for something which by contrast is thought, even though it is thought apparently instantaneously transformed into action, or, to reverse Keats's formulation of negative capability, 'action which is used as a substitute for thought and not action which is used as a prelude to thought'. Keats, it will be remembered, speaks of the capacity for tolerating half-truths and mysteries as essential for the language of achievement in contrast to thinking as a substitute for action. This differentiation of row A from column 6 seems potentially to be a useful aid to assessment of psycho-analytical experience provided it is used in situations other than the session during which analysand and analyst are engaged in psycho-analytic practice. As with row C, the column 6 categories could themselves be extended, using a grid system for that category itself. The uses to which I put the Grid, which I shall now illustrate, may serve as more effective than further explanation.

First, I will give some examples of row C constructs which I have chosen because they have a vivid pictorial quality; they are well known and the first is Freud's own famous

1 choice, *the Oedipus myth*. As it is well known I do not propose to take time on it except to stress the part played by Tiresias and the Sphinx in addition to the characters usually regarded as constituting the central feature of the story—the old King, his Queen Jocasta and Oedipus.

2 In the *Royal Cemetery at Ur*, approximately 3500 BC, the King was laid to rest. As far as the scene can be reconstructed from the excavations carried out by the joint expedition of the British Museum and the Museum of the University of Pennsylvania, included in the ceremony was a procession of the notables of the monarch's court into a specially prepared pit. There, clothed in the splendour of their jewels and finery they took a potion of a narcotic drug, conjectured to be hashish; to the accompaniment of music the pit, with its occupants in position, was then filled in with earth.

The site chosen for this cemetery was the city's refuse heap. We may assume that the magic performed that day was held to have sanctified the ground chosen and thus to have overlaid not only the real rubbish deposited on that site but also the view, if it existed, that the human remains were rubbish and that the appropriate place for the disposal of rubbish was the rubbish heap. Sanctification made the ground desirable for those who sought a resting place of magic property for their own dead rubbish. Thus the sanctified place, together with the sanctity which made it desirable, came in the course of time to lose its virtue as it became vulgarized, too full for further burials, and finally reverted to its former use.

Some five hundred years later a different kind of procession took place at the same site. Unless psycho-analysis develops a technique analogous to that of archaeology we shall not know what was in the hearts and minds of those courtiers of Ur, Abraham's City, when they walked into that death pit, took their potion and died. It may be easier to guess 3 what was in the minds of *the plunderers* who became so active during the Third Dynasty. Five hundred years was not long in those days and the mental climate in which that court, with its wealth about it, chose to accompany its king cannot have been so completely dissipated that the tomb robbers could be without fear that they might meet the spirits of the Dead in the course of their adventure. The Royal mourners demonstrated the power of Religion, Ritual, Magic, Drugs. The plunderers demonstrated the power of gain, and we should perhaps accord them a high position in the Pantheon of Scientific Fame as the forerunners of Science in the domain more usually left in the possession of Magic, Religion and the Dead.

This reconstruction is a transformation of the archaeological report on the joint expedition to form the verbal counterpart of two visual images, burial and plunder. For convenience I transform burial to A; plunder to B. I propose to use the two images A and B to represent the entire domain in which it is usual for psycho-analysts to operate. The visual images represented by A and B impose a degree of rigidity and immobility on the elements composing the pictures. If we *dis*articulate the images, the elements composing them are freed and the patterns become incoherent elements on which one can impose a pattern which makes order appear where none existed before. The facts worth attention are those which introduce order into this complexity. I have done this by introducing a five-hundred-year gap which separates these two facts in a relatively meaningful way: order has been introduced though it may not seem to add much to what is known. The fact which I have introduced is an idea of dividing the elements into two—those occurring in say 3500 BC and those occurring in 3000 BC. Separating the elements, dividing them into two categories or sets labelled respectively 3500 BC and 3000 BC may make the elements meaningful.

It is possible that that categorization, effected by introducing an idea of time as the instrument by which the separation and selection is effected, yields a train of thought of this kind: how powerful must be the force, emotional, cultural, religious, which can impose on a group of people a course of action certain to lead to their death, without their apparently being deterred by what is so certain. Is there any equivalent force in operation today which could obscure or conceal a fact as dangerous to us and as apparent to our posterity as the death of the men and women who proceeded into the death pit appears certain to us? A child can do something as dangerous to its life: are we correct if we assume it is ignorance? Would we be correct to assume that it is something unknown, more dynamic than ignorance which impelled it on a course certain to lead to its death? Is it the ignorance of the childhood of the race which is amply sufficient to explain the death of the Royal Court of Ur? Or is there some force for which we require a name—like 'religion' —because 'ignorance' is not pointing or denoting a sufficiently dynamic force?

Reciprocally, should we regard the 3000 BC group as demonstrating the power of a prospect of wealth to overwhelm the fears of the tomb robbers? As I have said, the space of five hundred years would then be scarcely long enough to dim appreciably the fears of the forces which had led to the death march of the ancient court. What courage would be required to brave those murderous forces—or was it simply a love of gain? How did the robbers come by the knowledge which enabled them, five hundred years after the event, to sink the shafts into the earth with such accuracy as to find the Queen' s Tomb? Was it luck? Should we regard our religious hierarchy as spiritual descendants of the priests of Ur? Should we erect monuments to the plunderers of the Royal Tombs as Pioneers of Science, as scientific as our scientists? Or should we consider today's scientists as deserving of obloquy for their cupidity?

The A group seem to have each taken a narcotic drug before they were buried alive. Was that the only drug, conjectured to be hashish, or was there some much more powerful force, more deserving of the title of 'drug', which was operating even before the death of the monarch?

What was the drug taken at B? Was it curiosity? When we

consider the hostility attributed to the deity both with regard
4 to the Tree of Knowledge in the *Garden of Eden*, and
expressed by the confusion of Tongues in the myth of the
5 building of the *Tower of Babel*, the question becomes significant. This and other points will be discussed further when we consider omnipotence.

The five stories, numbered in the margin, constitute a verbal picture gallery. They provide me, with such few additions as I pick up from my general reading, with models for almost any aspect of the emotional situations I can see for myself in that domain where practical psycho-analysis and psycho-analytic theories intersect.

The Ur reconstructions are based on those of Sir Leonard Woolley: I think they conveniently adumbrate the whole emotional domain with which psycho-analysts have to deal in romantically primitive and therefore compressed terms. [Historical writers, reconstructing what Freud calls historical truth for lack of psycho-analytic history, have to leave out the people—Hamlet without the Prince. *See* Sir Frederick Powicke, *The Lord Edward*.]

In addition to the five stories mentioned I include the *Death of Palinurus* (Virgil, Aeneid Book V) [see page 29].

Religious formulations which divide good and evil do not possess the significance of the undivided principle residing in the same deity. In the practice of psycho-analysis I am convinced that the emotional experience can be discerned as a constantly changing pattern of emotional experience. If the psycho-analyst develops his capacity to intuit these experiences he can become aware that there are certain experiences which are constantly conjoined and that these constant conjunctions are themselves experienced as repeated conjunctions. These constant conjunctions become manifest to the psycho-analyst after a period of time (provided he resists an irritable searching after certainty) as a sensuous kaleidoscopic change; the sensuous change will bear a resemblance to elements of the C categories that are found amongst his models.

I am aware that it may seem that I am suggesting that the psycho-analyst should engage painfully on the elaborations that he then strives to match against his emotional experience in his sessions. This is directly contrary to fact. His own analysis should have put him in reach of denuding himself of his memory and desires. The formation of his own private battery of C category sensuous elements—myths, images and so on—is carried through away from any psycho-analytic session, though it may be genetically related to his work sessions. Once formed it does not matter how often and how variously he re-forms these C-category elements provided he conforms to the discipline of denuding himself of memories and desires and, as soon as he can, of his tendency to understand. Darwin expressed one aspect of this discipline when he stated to his wife (as she reported in the appendix to his autobiography) that 'it is fatal to reason whilst observing, though so necessary beforehand and so useful afterwards'. The opacity of 'understanding' and its plausibility as an aim of the psycho-analyst tend to hide the danger of precosity and prematurity.

The more the Grid, or something more effective, is studied, the clearer will it become that the psycho-analyst will not only have to develop his power to intuit but he will need to keep it in good repair in the way, analogously, that the eye surgeon must keep the small muscles of his hands in perfect order. It is useless to have an armament of theories and to be insensitive to the facts which have to be interpreted. Classical, Kleinian, or other theories present no difficulties in practice. The psycho-analyst is aware of Freud's principle that matters which are observed must be called by their proper names. If he witnesses certain facts he is under an obligation to state his evidence; equally, he must not report what he does not see. Otherwise he is guilty of fraud.

For the purpose of this communication I propose to give a factual account of a one-time patient who attended regularly for a psycho-analytic course. I categorize it as a fairly sophisticated account; so I label it F3. The man had, I understood, an academically successful career until he left school and joined a commercial firm as a research chemist with good prospects and a safe job. An admiring relative was going to pay the fees. He was well acquainted with psycho-analytic circles and had slight knowledge of me but I did not know how much. He lay on the couch and lapsed into silence. I waited and after a few minutes asked him what he was thinking about. He did not reply. I became aware after a further silence that he was not in fact being silent—he was stammering. Of course, I thought, I should have realized that; he had told me he had a stammer which sometimes became so intense that for a period he could not say anything. I listened intently. (It was directed attention so I call it column 4 row B? row C?) He would breathe deeply, pause, let out his breath and start again. Each time he would draw in his breath suddenly and sharply and then suddenly let it out again as if experiencing considerable relief. I could make nothing of it. After a few moments he became silent again.

After a further pause I realized I had been listening in the expectation that he would speak and not listening to what I could hear. At first my impression was that he was straining to pass a motion. Again he relapsed into a silence. This time it was broken by sounds as if he were swallowing, perhaps nearly retching. I drew his attention to the facts and said that they could, if I ignored all impressions other than sound, be evidence of activity at both ends of his alimentary canal. He agreed verbally but as if the 'stammer' continued; as nearly as I can represent it he breathed out sharply 'Hah, hah, just . . . hah . . . a problem . . . hah . . . hah . . . in ph . . . huh . . . her . . . nation.' I said he seemed to be making both a sarcastic comment on what was taking place—his 'stammer' and my interpretation. He then said, after a preliminary check in his voice but not in his lips, 'I think you are quite right.' Fear of further difficulty made him talk hurriedly, stop quickly as if exhausted and remain silent.

In this brief account of one part of one session I shall assume that the narrative is as nearly truthful as I can make it. I do not make notes in a session or afterwards so that it is open to anyone to object that the account cannot be true. I am sure it would be even less true if mechanisms had been devised which seemed to record and repeat whatever was to be thus preserved (F3). But I have already categorized my attention to the patient as being suitably represented by category F4. Either the categories are badly drawn up and unsuitable for the load I am trying to make the Grid carry, or my assessment of the material is faulty or, more likely than either, both are true. Anyone who examines the Grid both on psycho-analytic grounds and for scientific methodological rigour will be dissatisfied. Too much must not be expected of human beings attempting discipline with a method which is hardly a hundred years old. J. O. Wisdom has been critical, but rightly appreciative, of Guntrip's attempt to bring methodological standards to bear on psycho-analysis. As I am not able to offer any suggestions for improvement I shall leave the unsatisfactory formulations alone and comfort myself that I am resisting the temptation to reach irritably 'after fact and reason' through my not being 'capable of being in uncertainties, mysteries, doubts'.

The most striking feature of the episode was the discovery of the extent to which I began to feel the futility and exasperation of sitting waiting for a man to tell me what he wanted when he would not speak at all. This was almost at once followed by astonishment that apparently he could not talk—that his stammer was so severe. I felt no wiser and no nearer to thinking of any interpretation which was likely to have the effect which I had always understood good interpretations to have. One of my colleagues once told me he had given the patient all the interpretations known to psycho-analysis without any effect whatever. Allowing for exaggeration I could sympathize with his feelings. Today they are my familiars, but two points help—these feelings are no longer strange to me and I do not quite so easily allow myself to be deafened by the uproar of what the patient is *not* saying or doing. The danger is not that some possible interpretation known to psycho-analysis is not known to the overburdened psycho-analyst, but that he is so distracted by particular instances masquerading as the discovery of a new general theory that he cannot observe the facts. Although I have now for many years devoted myself to the practice of analysis, as opposed to talking about it, I am constantly surprised by the extent to which I fail in this apparently simple and yet rewarding task. In fact, it took me a very long time to become convinced of the need to denude myself of memory and desire, and longer still before I appreciated the vicious effect on observation that was exerted by a need to understand. The latter is a particular instance of the obtrusion of desire which is liable to rationalization by psycho-analysts. It may be as well to mention some features which contribute to the difficulties of any psycho-analyst disposed to try this discipline. It appears to be easy. It is contrary to the conventions of ordinary medical practice to be unaware of so many and such apparently important items in the family and individual history, and it would leave the psycho-analyst open to attack on the grounds of negligence should something go wrong. The mass of evidence which becomes available in contact with the personality of the analysand makes it necessary to tolerate the constant oscillation from paranoid-schizoid to depressive position, or from patience to security which I suggest as more accurate descriptions of the psycho-analyst's fluctuations.

The resolve not to allow myself to be distracted by the facts about the patient which I did not know, but thought I might be expected to know, proved a great, though at times guilty, relief. I soon extended the procedure through all my practice, always, it seemed, with advantage. I cannot describe the process in detail, though with regard to the Grid I found the thought required, whether to satisfy myself, which I did not succeed in doing, of the soundness of my estimate of what had taken place, or to effect some improvement in the Grid as an instrument, itself led to a great clarification of my thinking both generally and with regard to the particular patient with whose problem I was concerned. This advantage, like others, did not quickly become clear to me. The gradual and imperceptible nature of the progress contributes to the difficulty in my knowing how to proceed in order to pass on the nature of the experience to colleagues. Being wise after the event, it surprises me how often the attempts to clarify my experience would lead to the emergence of what seemed a bright idea and how often the bright idea failed to materialize in practice. At first I was outraged by this and wanted to distort the evidence to conform to my hunch. This breaking of my own rules was always a failure and contributed to a sense of fraudulence. It took some hardihood and misery to say goodbye to any of my brain-children. I was hardened in my resolve to do so by the discovery that the bright idea shared the quality which is displayed in a dream when it appears to disappear not so much bit by bit, but completely and as a whole. It was at about the same time that I realized that the same idea could reappear as suddenly and as completely. I hoped that full attention to the analysand would act as the trigger which would start off the forgotten, but hopefully appropriate, thought. None the less it is a sad thing to have to abandon one's bright ideas before ever having discovered how bright they were.

I am concerned here to write some of the thoughts stimulated by this and other sessions round about this time. This is not so much a report—the kind of event which I would categorize by column 3—as a reverie *now* about the kind of reveries I learnt to indulge in these early days of psychoanalytic practice. The effect of my own analysis was that it diminished the obstructive force of unconscious memories and though I acquired new ones, usually believed to be the theories of my analyst, the effects of such recently acquired memories were of a different kind from those usually characterized as inhibitions; these last could be more fruitfully, though more vaguely, described as column 2 categories—that is to say, psycho-analytical objects feared as liable to trigger off developments of a catastrophic nature, to initiate 'catastrophic change'. Their nature may well be exemplified by two descriptions which cannot possibly be described as psycho-analytical.

The first is that in which Poincaré, the mathematician, describes, in his *Science and Method*, the psychological accompaniment of elaborating creatively a mathematical formula. I shall not quote it again because I have already quoted it so often as to risk pushing it towards becoming a ritual, a recital in scientific terms of a formula intended to keep at bay the development, in today's cant terms of the political dictator, of 'dangerous thoughts'.

The second is a quotation from the autobiography of Max Planck of a discovery which was only incidental to his work with mechanical quanta. 'It is one of the most painful experiences of my entire life that I have but seldom—in fact, I might say, never—succeeded in gaining universal recognition for a new result, the truth of which I could demonstrate by a conclusive, albeit only theoretical proof. . . . This experience gave me also an opportunity to learn a fact—a remarkable one in my opinion: a new scientific truth does not triumph by convincing its opponents and making them see the light, but rather because its opponents eventually die, and a new generation grows up that is familiar with it'.

After I had discovered in the course of my work with all members of my practice the obstructive quality of preconceptions, the patient's analysis became more lifelike. It did not matter whether the preconceptions had sprung from what I had consciously and unconsciously gathered from the contact with the patient, or whether it was something I had heard in another context, or whether it was some psycho-analytic theory. The increase in lifelike quality was associated with an increased readiness to perceive non-verbal quality. As I became more practised at ignoring—or as Freud put it 'artificially blinding myself'—certain memories and desires, I found the patient's attempts to speak less able to demand my attention. There he lay, spluttering and farting and sucking away with his lips, and never a word of English. Had he been in command of the knowledge one would expect of a man of his age, I should say it was a perfect symphony concert of rude noises. It was, had I realized it earlier, a virtuoso performance. For some time I made interpretations appropriate to the idea that the noises were being made by a single mouth but I could be aware, in the course of my daily cogitations—the occasions for which I had elaborated the Grid—that this idea was related to an assumption that a personality corresponds to the visible anatomical structures of the person. There used in my childhood to be a character known as the one-man-band. With an arrangement of pulleys, strings, a drum and a sort of harmonium he could be kicking up his heels, waving his arms, throwing his head back violently and suddenly, and thereby putting up a tolerable imitation of a musical performance, sounding his drum with his forehead, ringing a bell with his occiput and so forth. For some reason I could not understand, I was not allowed to watch this performance but used to be hauled off as if from some indecent spectacle. I was reminded of this—another model for ephemeral purposes—as I dragged myself into contact with the patient. After a time I said it sounded as if his mouth, his anus, his throat, were all engaged in a struggle for attention, for who should be supreme. 'Fff . . .', he replied, 'F.f.f . . . Ffphonation' , he finally exploded. 'It sounds' he said with increasing freedom 'as if they were trying to settle who was top. But . . .' and again he became inarticulate. For a moment or two he repeated noises which I was quite used to hearing. The pattern of sound was very distinct but though I felt sure it resembled something I was still unable to suggest any further interpretation. I said, 'These different parts of the anatomy seem each to have a personality, like a real person, and each to be ambitious to make use of your "phonation"'. 'Like trying to get hold of the microphone and keep all others out', he said. I thought of 'internal objects' (F4) but could not see that this theory met the difficulty of which I had been vaguely conscious before when speaking of what was to be considered as marking the boundaries of the personality. I could not feel sure that the patient felt that these 'objects' were inside him. As he was speaking they might as well have been 'outside' him. I asked him if he felt they were outside. He continued easily and fluently about a companion of whose intelligence he had very great doubts. He said he was afraid he might have to work with him as his partner on an explosive project and that might be extremely dangerous. Once before, a man had caused an explosion in the laboratory which seemed to fragment every glass vessel in the room. They might both have been killed. As it was, his companion had lost an eye. He did not want to lose his. He stopped, leaving me somewhat surprised by such a long speech. There was no sign of impediment; nor could I see any impediment to the expression of a copious flow of interpretations which was occurring to me. I would have been reduced to stammering myself if I had even tried to formulate them. I said he was expressing his anxiety about having to come for an analysis to a psycho-analyst whose intelligence was as limited as my own. Compared to Doctor X, a very good psycho-analyst whom he knew, I was felt to be about as intelligent as a bottle compared to a breast. 'Contrariwise', he interrupted. I then said he felt the bottle to be at least efficient compared with the human being with whom he shared the laboratory. I said the envy with which the eyes regarded the intercourse had led to an explosive destruction of the eye and the glass vessels. He began to stammer again and there was no further verbal communication. The session ended but not before I had noticed that this time no sound came from his lips. The movement of his lips was most pronounced and most peculiar. As far as I could see from my position it was as if the muscles of the mouth were fibrillating in a way which I have known only in heart muscle and associated with the lipidoses. I could not see how this effect was produced. Though I was for a number of reasons suspicious of this patient and was careful not to allow symptoms to escape notice, I did not see this symptom recur. However, it alerted me to the necessity for watching for transformations of problems of personality into systems with which they are not usually associated. In so far as developments of either one's own or the analysand's outlook can be traced to certain nodal events (in fact I am convinced it cannot), it forms a convenient fiction which may be used for separating one part of a discussion from another.

I have gathered together my cogitations on this and other cases which I was psycho-analysing at that time without a temporal or spatial framework. A problem which seemed to be insoluble, or to be assumed to be solved by being linked to an extremely inadequate solution, was that presented by the liar. Having had experience of the creations of someone who was in fact notorious enough in his capacity as a liar to be known diagnostically as a pathological liar—a diagnosis that begs all the questions but becomes more manageable if it is regarded as a definitory hypothesis (D, E, F1)—I found I had to respect what, had he been a writer of fiction, would have been regarded as great gifts of imagination. The situation became more complex when I found it necessary to give papers, write reports and teach. What a gift, what a blessing I thought it would have been to be a born liar! No sooner had I thought it than I realized that I was deploring the lack of the one characteristic which is in fact inborn though it had to wait, as always, for the genius to reach its full capacity. In this case the genius, or group genius, who invented speech released the liar from his bondage. The point was brought home by a veterinary surgeon who, on being asked whether it was not a great handicap to have patients who could not say what they were complaining of, replied that it was made up for by the fact that they could not lie either. My stammerer was on certain occasions in that position: he lacked the gift of language! And even when he could talk his whole prejudice was to speak the truth. I did not at first realize the handicap under which he laboured when, as was often the case, he wished to preserve a private life *and* have a psycho-analysis. For convenience, the assumption of priority of deception as the senior function, has some value for emphasizing a possibility usually disregarded. In fact I claim no value for this idea other than that of drawing attention to one of the inherent problems of psycho-analysis. Communication, not even verbal communication, was designed for the purpose of psycho-analysis as a method of scientific investigation of the personality. Many methods of investigation, religious, legal, philosophical, have been elaborated for the discovery of truth. The lot of psycho-analysis has been to expose the hollowness of the pretensions of all these disciplines. As far as possible we need to find some method by which we do not fall into the same pit. At the outset there is a difficulty—for we do not purport to dictate, even suppose we could, how anyone can be made to use psycho-analysis for scientific purposes only. Anyone is free to undergo a training and, once qualified, use his qualification for any purpose he chooses. The analysand can persist in courses of action which led to his original departure from health and which will inevitably undo any growth which psycho-analysis might promote. The patient I have selected as a point of discussion was one who by training, ability and prejudice was particularly likely to pursue his analysis to develop his scientific flair.

I shall begin with the choice of two apparently different types of liar. One I shall call the 'charming' liar, the other the 'poisonous' liar. The terms have an advantage in being known in conversational English and are usually reserved for people who symptomatically are very different. This superficial difference soon tends to declare its superficiality. Both are peculiar in the significance they share socially. Indeed, a phrase which has come into use recently shows that the presence of both psychological trends operates in the very highest circles to such an extent that an almost scientific term has had to be invented, namely, 'the credibility gap'. The chief reason why these trends need to be recognized is because they appear to have, borrowing a biological term, a toxic effect on mental development. I am not speaking only of individual mental development, though that is naturally the central concern of psycho-analysts, but the mental or psychological or moral development of whole groups. This is not the place to discuss the group aspect of this problem but I think psycho-analysts will ignore this extension of the individual to their peril. But . . . why did my patient stammer? Certainly I would have been hesitant about regarding him as falling into either of the two named categories. He was mischievous in a pleasant way, he was kind and considerate. He was the victim of much cruelty, a fact of which he was unaware and for which I was dependent on hearsay.

As the analysis proceeded I was able to interpret the stammer as part of a dramatic presentation of three people in the room. The most obvious trio was of course Father, Mother, Child. The closest representation of this depended on the actual session. I have found no way in which it is possible to pass on to someone who was not there the changes constantly occurring in the sessions as a whole or those occurring in any single session. Naturally psycho-analytic colleagues would like to have evidence; naturally I would like to give evidence. But with the passage of time I am convinced that there is no substitute for psycho-analysis.

The following is an attempt to indicate the direction in which evidence is to be found. Let us assume that the psycho-analyst has managed to rid himself of the clamour of psycho-analytical gang warfare, the pressures of the daily problems of individual survival, to a point where it is relatively quiet in the office. The man of whom I am writing was often speechless for very considerable periods. As I have already indicated, my preconceptions—now I would call them my psycho-analytic and other prejudices—made it difficult for me, as it was for him, to tolerate the silence. As I became more able to silence my prejudices, I also became able to be aware of the evidence that was there rather than to regret the evidence that was not. As my ears became used to the silence, little sounds became easier to hear. I was reminded of an analogy which Freud used where he wrote of having artificially to blind himself in order to direct the faintest glimmer of light in a very dark situation. Transforming this I used the analogy to consider the importance of 'artificial silence' in order to hear very 'faint noises'. It worked. I began to hear sounds which would formerly have passed unnoticed.

My object in giving these accounts is their value in providing verbal formulations of visual images. The visual image, as television and the movies have shown, has great power of lateral communication. Verbal communication, or at least the written form, depending on the durability of the medium, has greater staying power, as witnessed by the Homeric poems, the code of Hammurabi, Virgil and, in recent times, Shakespeare. When it comes to phonation (it will be remembered that when my patient did vocalize he did it with great accuracy and precision and used that term) the situation is more complex. Tacitus gives a good general description of the function of the bard in the Germanic tribe; he also gives particular descriptions of the part played by Percennius after the death of Augustus Caesar. Should you wonder what this has to do with psycho-analysis, I suggest that you let your curiosity lead you to listen to recordings—I was able to study some which I borrowed from the British Broadcasting Corporation—of Hitler's speeches made at rallies in Nüremberg. The emotional forces active in the time of Tacitus are *still* active. I am fortunate in not understanding German and therefore was not distracted by the element of articulate speech to a point where I could not hear the phonation or be unaware of the beta-elements. I define these as elements which lie outside the spectrum of 'thought'.

The dilemma for the psycho-analyst is this: I do not believe, and nor does anyone else who has had close contact with men in battle conditions, prisoners of war or civilians in similar stress, that the feelings of men and women either as individuals or as members of a group have changed; they are dormant. Often they are covered by a veneer of civilization which, however, does not conceal though it may disguise the forces beneath. Sometimes it becomes clear to the psycho-analyst that the boundaries of the person do not correspond to the person' s anatomical structure. Melanie Klein, as I understood her to say, did not think that there was any mystery about apparently concerted movements in a group of analysands beyond what could be explained by transference relationship with the same analyst. I think we should keep an open mind. I do not feel any need to postulate 'extra-sensory' perception, a herd instinct as Wilfred Trotter did, or a group unconscious as Jung did. I think, however, that there may well be some analogue in the personality to the capillary blood system which in ordinary conditions is dormant but in extraordinary conditions may dilate as in surgical shock. The analogy would be such hyperstimulation of the individual 'groupishness' that his capacity for conscious, sophisticated behaviour seeps away into his 'unconscious'. Freud considered that there might be substance in Weismann' s theory of the individual personality as subordinate to the germ plasm. (Standard Edition, Vol. XIV, page 125). There are certainly situations in which the analysis seems to be on the periphery of the main theme: the investigation continues but it is difficult to suppose that the field being investigated is of real consequence; yet the patient comes, though he complains of the futility of the procedure. The complaint suggests awareness of some preoccupation which is not futile. If the patient were a child who goes to a parent and asks, 'What shall I do now?' it would be easier to understand. But he is not a child and the psycho-analyst does not purport to suggest solutions for such problems. Why then does the analysand behave as if he were? It may be that the analysand has developed, the psycho-analyst has developed, and the problems have developed the fastest of all—so fast that they have outgrown psycho-analysis itself. That is a guess but there are others. I do not limit myself to one 'favoured' solution. Freud may have been on the wrong tack, or, as I think more likely, man, even Freud, cannot possibly do more than scratch the surface in the short time available to him. There is also a possibility that the training, the teaching, is both too good and too bad. It is so good that it becomes second nature to go and find some expert to work out the problem. It is so bad that all initiative, all capacity for finding out is destroyed. The problem, the object of curiosity, has to be approached symmetrically. 'Too good' and 'too bad' is not a formulation of a conflict; it is a formulation of a symmetrical relationship. It is analogous, in the domain of personality, to bifocal vision in the domain of visual inquiry. In sensuous experience the eyes are focused, brought to a point where they 'meet'. The 'apparatus' of intuition cannot be expressed in the simple terms available to formulation of homogeneous sensuous experience. Real and imaginary only supplement each other when they do not meet, when it is known that two parallel lives in the domain of sensuous experience meet, but in the domain of personality they become symmetrical.

Freud's second thoughts about using the term 'interpretation' when 'construction' would appear to be more apposite is certainly compatible with, though I could hardly regard it as confirmatory of, my idea that for some purposes for which analysts use interpretations they require constructions, and that these constructions are essential instruments for the demonstration of symmetry. A sensuous component of this apparatus is the visual image. The C elements I have sketched out differ from the interpretation, which is usually monovalent, whereas the construction (C element) is polyvalent and is faster than the F or G formulations though it may not be faster than the H formulations if and when they can be discovered. This is a matter of great practical consequence when the psycho-analyst has to cope with primitive material. The analysand operating on a primitive level comes close to acting on the principle of 'act first, think later'. Usually the analysand in such an episode is acting in relationship with the analyst as if, to put it in a mixture of real and imaginary terms, an extremely active, flexible and speedy unconscious were being pursued by a slow, rigid, lumbering conscious.

I must now take up in some detail a word I often use, in common with most psycho-analysts—'analogy'. I have in fact used analogy in describing the conscious as lumbering after the unconscious. I used it without acknowledgement because the form is disguised (revealed?) as a silent metaphor; its use is disguised. Sometimes the metaphor has become so much a part of conversational English that it is 'dead'—unless, as Fowler points out, it is brought to life by juxtaposition with another metaphor whose inappropriateness, non-homogeneity, sends a galvanic-like flutter through it. As I have already pointed out, confusion can occur because attention is given to the two images used in the analogy, and not, which is the important point, the relationship between them. Vaihinger exaggerated the relationship, not surprisingly, into a philosophical system. Freud spoke of this contribution in 'The Future of an Illusion' . Bringing to bear the construction, the polyvalent weapon of symmetry, I would suggest that we need to consider the future of an analogy, the future of an 'illusion', the future of 'transference' which is the name given by psycho-analysts to a particular and potent form of relationship. If one could arrange the term, spectrum-wise, in ascending power of emotional drive it could be: generation → analogy → transference → delusion → illusion → group illusion → hallucination → asymmetry → degeneration. C elements are used to provide anchorage for the relationship—mouth is one anchor, breast is the other. Both of these terms have been treated as if they were the essential features of the analogy. It is exactly this point that marks the divergence of the path of growth from the path of decay. The breast and the mouth are only important in so far as they serve to define the bridge between the two. When the 'anchors' usurp the importance which belongs to the qualities which they should be imparting to the bridge, growth is impaired. The man with the stammer was 'held' because he could not progress beyond the importance of defecation, urination, the mouth as an object to be sensuously gratified by the tongue and vice versa.

The interpretation or construction produced by the psycho-analyst depends on the intuitive link between analysand and analyst. As it is constantly imperilled by deliberate attacks, its essential frailty and ordinary fatigue, it needs to be protected and maintained. The object of the Grid is to provide a mental gymnastic tool. It can be used in relative isolation from attack and cannot do harm so long as it is not allowed to intrude into the relationship between analysand and the analyst as by the elaboration of some theory about the patient which is then stored up and used as something which can be discharged like a missile in a battle.

What I have said of the function of the anchors in an analogy will show how acute the attention needs to be. The point is emphasized by certain patients whose sending and receiving of signals depends on the use of a very narrow waveband. The message sent by the analyst is either correctly metred or it is not received. Similarly, the message sent by the analysand has to be received by the wide-band receiver as represented by symmetry. I have experienced this in its most acute form in the musician who has perfect pitch. I have also had to contend with it in a patient whose visual sense made it impossible for him to tolerate the slightest deviation from what was, in his opinion, the correct colour.

These facts require that the analyst should not allow himself to be restricted simply to the evidence provided by speech, but must he be restricted to the communication? Freud said it is better to avoid 'symbolic disguisings', but what about symbolic revelations? It may be the only kind of reception which is commensurate with the child's ability. Analysands often think they can afford an analysis. If the figures add up correctly according to the rules of their religious belief in the omnipotence of money, and if the power of financial rituals to control their anxieties are commensurate with their anxieties, they may be betrayed into an entirely erroneous belief that they can 'afford' a psychoanalysis.

Freud shows that while he regards belief in God as an illusion, he has no doubt about the reality of the illusion. The illusion must be taken seriously by psycho-analysts. In this particular sphere I think *interpretation* (as opposed to construction) of omnipotence is particularly unfortunate. It minimizes the constant conjunction which is the reality that is often so inadequately represented by the single term, 'omnipotence', or even the symmetrical version of it, 'omnipotence–helplessness'. The Palinurus story [see below] (which I think Virgil intended us to take seriously as part of religion and not just an epic poem, any more than Milton regarded Paradise Lost as an exercise in artistic virtuosity) provides a better 'construction' than any 'interpretation' or other invention to draw together the conjoined elements when 'omnipotence' is in question. The liar gives substance to his phantasies of omnipotence because, unlike speaking the truth, he does not simply record—he does something. Recording, speaking the truth, is merely to be an insignificant cog in the machinery. In effect this means that in the personality in which intolerance of frustration coexists with great ambition, greed tends to dominate and the 'result' dominates the greed. The 'end', or 'aim', or 'supposed aim', of an activity precipitates prematurity and precocity. It is difficult to accept real life because frustration is an essential feature of real life. In an extreme position it obstructs the development of thought. As Freud points out, the capacity for thought acts potentially by interposing delay between an impulse and its transformation into action, but it can also make the frustration, inseparable from translating thought into action, more bearable. The 'ambitious–intolerant conjunction' can then perpetuate itself; thought being replaced by omnipotence (which has no part in reality) tends thus to increase frustration, denies the personality such moderation of frustration as thought might provide, and impels towards violence such as robbery and murder. The premature acquisition of the supposed valuable object means that even a genuine valuable cannot be used to yield satisfaction because the maturity required to effect the transformation from potential to actual is missing. The term 'omnipotence', as contrasted with 'construction', such as the Palinurus story, is too abstract to give an idea of the reality to which the psycho-analyst attempts to draw attention. Omnipotence–omniscience–god, together with the symmetrical elements, helplessness–incomprehension–agnosticism, are the abstract statements of the basic group. I shall now introduce, instead of these abstract terms, the C version, a verbal formulation of a visual image.

The death of Palinurus

The anxieties of father Aeneas being allayed by Neptune, the fleet takes advantage of the calm following the storm; it is ordered to conform to the movements of the column steered by Palinurus.

The sailors go to sleep. Somnus seeks out Palinurus bringing the guiltless man bad dreams. Disguised as Phorbas he seats himself on the stern and proceeds to seduce Palinurus by pointing out that it is time for sleep, the seas are calm and favourable and that he, Phorbas, will take over the tiller allowing Palinurus to rest. Palinurus makes a very direct and contemptuous reply, scorning the suggestion that he would sleep when dealing with such a treacherous sea, or risk the life of his commander. He does not let go the tiller or take his eyes off the stars by which he steers.

The god then shakes the dews of Lethean forgetfulness over him and hurls him into the sea with such violence that Palinurus carries part of the stern with him. His comrades do not hear his calls for help and he is drowned.

Aeneas, finding the ship yawing, and saddened by the fecklessness of Palinurus, takes over the helm.

This model is one from which, according to the dictates of the material, the analyst can formulate a 'construction'. Interpretation, in the sense which Freud discards the term, may indeed be a useful preliminary, a prelude to the 'construction'. The symmetrical nature of the story makes possible the choice of any element to be the vertex, without alteration in the value of the function. Thus, the patient might be obtruding an anxiety about drugs; the analyst is offered a choice of drugs in this story. A patient may wish to obtrude a grievance about unfair treatment; again, the analyst has a choice of elements on which his attention might focus. The point I make is that the story helps to draw attention to the fact that certain elements are constantly conjoined; that fact may escape attention but for a model of this kind. The gap between the theory and the patient on the couch can be too great for relevance to be apparent, especially when the prejudice in favour of theory is too active. Equally, if there are not enough C models, the lack of theory may mean that the structure is not strong enough to carry the load it has to bear in practice.

The respect in which psycho-analysis seems to me to be seriously deficient is in models (C) of omnipotence–helplessness (F). As a result the constantly conjoined elements are recognized as isolated units which have relevance only on rare occasions and fail to stimulate a response when they should on occasions which are of more frequent occurrence. The deficiency may be more apparent than real. If the Eden and Babel myths are used for models for the omnipotent–helpless theme and reinforced by the riddling Sphinx of the Oedipus myth, the deficiency is lessened. The 'morality' of the deity may also be expanded by consideration of the views expressed in Chapter 2 of the *Baghavadgita*. Such models help a psycho-analyst to bridge the gap between a theory and the material which is manifest in the psycho-analytic experience.

It is assumed that the psycho-analyst considers that the sophisticated theoretical formulation (F) and the model (C) are legitimate transformations, each of the other. In other words, there are invariants present in the psycho-analytic experience and in the theoretical formulation. On the correctness of this assumption the genuineness of the psycho-analysis depends. I have described elsewhere that under projection a round pond and an avenue of trees on the ground can be represented by an ellipse and two converging lines on a piece of paper. In short, there are invariants in these two factually different objects—the pond and trees, and the drawing. What are the invariants if one object is the fountains of Rome and the other the score of a piece of music by Respighi?

I have given a summary in visual terms of Virgil's account of the death of Palinurus. What are the invariants common to this and to the stammerer on the couch? What are the rules which have to be obeyed if the analysand can reasonably be expected to understand the analyst and vice versa?

In the world of physics an orchestral performance appears to be transformable, given suitable apparatus, into wireless waves; these can be transformed back again so that another human being can assume he is listening to an orchestral performance. Can a modern English-speaking person be trained to understand the printed representation of Virgil, Aeneid, Book V, lines 827–871? Can a trained person intervene between the Latin formulation and an American in such a way that there is a carry-over of invariants common to the Latin poem and the English comprehension?

I cannot, even if I wanted to, answer these questions. Nor, as far as I know, can the Grid. But I have found, and think that others might likewise find, that the Grid could serve to provide a mental climbing frame on which the psycho-analyst could exercise his mental muscles. Even its defects could be turned to advantage.

Ezra Pound has been severely criticized for his translation of the classics such as his *Homage to Sextus Propertius*, the *Analects of Confucius*, and the *Classical Anthology*. It could easily be shown, perhaps too easily, that Pound was guilty of certain schoolboy howlers in his translations from the Latin. Since he is a human being there is no shortage of human frailty available for ammunition, the symmetrical approach being adulation and abuse. The practising psycho-analyst, the portrait painter, the musician, the sculptor, all have to 'see' and demonstrate, so that others may see, the truth which is usually ugly and frightening to the person to whom the truth is displayed. In the same way the ugly and frightening are usually believed, by the person to whom they are displayed, to be identical with the truth.

∮ It takes a genius, a Faraday, to demonstrate the reality of electricity so that people of less messianic capacity can understand so much that they can switch on an electric light.

It takes a mystic to demonstrate the existence of God so that people who lack that endowment can understand enough to know when and how to switch on the appropriate ritual and employ the correct magic.

It takes a Freud to demonstrate the reality of emotional resources to such a point that people who have not such capacity can nevertheless receive the communications which demonstrate the resources and make them available.

So-called Scientific Laws are vulgarizations of that which the scientific mystic can achieve directly. Religious dogmata are similarly vulgarizations of that which the religious mystic can achieve directly.

The function of the Establishment, Scientific and Religious, is to protect the mystic from destruction and the group from the disruptive effects of the mystic. The Grid, like a primitive scheme of electrical switches, wires and so forth, is intended to help preserve psycho-analysis from being destroyed 'in its infancy', and the group, which has the misfortune to harbour such a lusty child, from disintegrating as a result of the uncontrolled and undirected vigour of the infant. As is the way with infants it can impress its environment both with its power and helplessness. ∮

The total description between ∮ and ∮ is by way of a pictorial simplification, and therefore an inevitable distortion, of the facts to be represented. Either the description becomes, like so much mathematics, indistinguishable from a meaningless manipulation of symbols, or it gains in psychological digestibility at the expense of scientific vigour. Psycho-analysis has not reached a point where it can be communicated without the presence of the objects which have to be demonstrated. In short, the object being interpreted, for which the construction is being elaborated, must be present at the time when its presence is supposed to be made manifest by the 'construction'. A microscopist cannot be constructing his microscope while he is looking through it—though he may be adjusting his powers of observation to its defects. The Grid is to be used in the process of this period of preparation, not as a substitute for observation or psycho-analysis but as a prelude to it.

CAESURA

SOURCES

S. Freud, *Inhibitions, Symptoms and Anxiety.*

'There is much more continuity between intra-uterine life and earliest infancy than the impressive caesura of the act of birth allows us to believe.'

M. Buber, *I and Thou.*

'The prenatal life of the child is a pure natural association, a flowing toward each other, a bodily reciprocity; and the life horizon of the developing being appears uniquely inscribed, and yet also not inscribed, in that of the being that carries it; for the womb in which it dwells is not solely that of the human mother.'

V. C. Walsh, Preface to *Introduction to Contemporary Microeconomics.*

'If one leaves a happy, spirited discussion with friends about currently debated topics . . . to get down to the job of arranging introductory lectures on the subject for a large audience, one may be struck by a certain oddity. The two worlds seem to have no intersection.'

M. Buber, *I and Thou.*

'Every developing human child rests, like all developing beings, in the womb of the great mother—the undifferentiated, not yet formed primal world. From this it detaches itself to enter a personal life, and it is only in dark hours when we slip out of this again (as happens even to the healthy, night after night) that we are close to her again. But this detachment is not sudden . . . like that from the bodily mother.'

M. Buber, *I and Thou.*

'From the glowing darkness of the chaos he has stepped into the cool and light creation without immediately possessing it. . . .'

S. Freud, Letter to Lou Andreas Salomé from Letters of 1873–1939.

'I know that in writing I have to blind myself artificially in order to focus all the light on one dark spot. . . .'

St John of the Cross, *Ascent of Mount Carmel.*

'The memory must also strip itself of all those forms and kinds of knowledge, that it may unite itself with God in hope.'

S. Freud, Letter to Lou Andreas Salomé from Letters of 1873–1939.

'. . . renouncing cohesion, harmony, edifying effects and everything which you call the symbolic element. . . .'

M. Buber, *I and Thou*. (Reference to Jewish myth).

'. . . in his mother's womb man knows the universe and forgets it at birth.'

St John of the Cross, *Ascent of Mount Carmel*.

'. . . the love which the memory always has for other forms and kinds of knowledge which are of supernatural things, such as visions, revelations, locutions and feelings which come in a supernatural way. When these things have passed through the soul, there is wont to remain impressed upon it some image, form, figure or idea, whether in the soul or in the memory of fancy, at times very vividly and effectively. Concerning these images it is also needful to give advice lest the memory becomes encumbered with them and they be a hindrance to its union with God in perfect and pure hope.'

The foregoing quotations were made from the vertex of different disciplines, at different times and in different languages. They delineate the universe of discourse within which this paper is confined.

Psycho-analysis is concerned with the domain of ideas; included are thoughts and feelings of all kinds. Although it could be described as a limited domain, a limited human activity, its scope nevertheless is vast when one considers *all* thoughts, feelings and ideas which are presented to us in the course of our work. In the physical sciences the human being is dealing with a physical material: psycho-analysts are concerned with characters, personalities, thoughts, ideas and feelings. But whatever the discipline there is a primitive, fundamental, unalterable and basic line—the truth. 'What is truth?' said jesting Pilate, according to Francis Bacon, and would not wait for an answer. *We* probably cannot wait for an answer, because we have not the time. Nevertheless, that is what we are concerned with—inescapably and unavoidably—even if we have no idea what is true and what is not. Since we are dealing with human characters we are also concerned with lies, deceptions, evasions, fictions, phantasies, visions, hallucinations—indeed, the list can be lengthened almost indefinitely.

In our relationships with analysands time is limited and choice inescapable. Which, of all the right interpretations, are we to choose to formulate? The analyst's freedom, though great, can be seen to be limited, at any rate on one boundary, by the need to be truthful, to give an interpretation which is a true one. If the analysand is sincere in his wish for treatment he likewise is limited; his free association should be as near to what he considers to be the truth as he can get. The course of the discussion itself between analyst and analysand may make it more possible to assess the degree of truth or falsity in any particular idea which is under scrutiny. But is one to call a feeling 'an idea'? It is a matter of definition, but we cannot exclude feelings any more than ideas from the field which we are to survey.

The embryologist speaks about 'optic pits' and 'auditory pits'. Is it possible for us, as psycho-analysts, to think that there may still be vestiges in the human being which would suggest a survival in the human mind, analogous to that in the human body, of evidence in the field of optics that once there were optic pits, or in the field of hearing that once there were auditory pits? Is there any part of the human mind which still betrays signs of an 'embryological' intuition, either visual or auditory?

This may seem to be an academic and unimportant matter—unless we think that there may be some truth in the statement made by Freud that there is some connection between post-natal thought and emotional life, and pre-natal life. To exaggerate the question for the sake of simplicity: are we to consider that the fetus thinks, or feels, or sees, or hears? If so, how primitive can these thoughts, or feelings, or ideas be?

Events sometimes take place in the consulting room, where there are present only myself and a grown man or woman, which suggest feelings that I could describe as envy, love, hate, sex, but which seem to have an intense and unformed character. It is convenient to fall back on physiology and anatomy to borrow ideas in order to express my feelings about some of these events; to think of some of the feelings which the patient is expressing as being subthalamic, or sympathetic, or para-sympathetic. There are occasions when the patient mentions some anxiety, fear, or a symptom (like blushing) briefly and unobtrusively, yet in a way which suggests that something is being mentioned in disguised and feeble terms because it is the best that the patient can do to give effect to feelings which are feared for their intensity, magnitude and obtrusiveness compared with those feelings which most people are used to regard as normal. Similarly, the patient may express a fear of the future which has many of the characteristics of a past which one thinks he could not possibly remember; nor can he remember the future because it has not yet happened. These things, so faintly expressed, may in truth be very powerful. I can imagine that there may be ideas which cannot be more powerfully expressed because they are buried in the future which has not happened, or buried in the past which is forgotten, and which can hardly be said to belong to what we call 'thought'. If you apply pressure to your eyeball you can see, in response to the physical pressure, what appears to be something which could only be a response of the optic apparatus. If that is so then maybe the optic pits respond to pressure even before the dramatic caesura of birth itself. From the point of view of the analyst the fact that the analysand is a grown man or woman can be so obtrusive, the evidence of the eyes so obtrusive, that it blinds him to feelings which are not so clearly presented to the optic apparatus.

Any attempt to classify the material with which we have to deal should be regarded as provisional, or transitive; that is to say, part of a process from one thought or idea or position to another—not a permanency, not a halting spot at which the investigation is ended. When the analyst is not sure what it is that is obtruding he is in the position of having an intuition without any corresponding concept—that intuition might be called 'blind'. Any concept, for example projective identification, is empty when it has no content. The problem for the practising analyst is how to match his hunch, or his intuition, or his suspicion, with some formulation, some conceptual statement. He has to do that *before* he can give an interpretation. The analyst's role, in other words, is one which inevitably involves the use of transitive ideas or ideas in transit. The analysand, likewise, is attempting through his free associations to formulate an experience of which he is aware.

As things are at present, giving an interpretation means that the analyst has to be capable of verbalizing a statement of his senses, his intuitions and his primitive reactions to what the patient says. This statement has to be effective as a physical act is effective. The analysand's difficulties, already great enough, are increased by his being limited to what little he can in fact do even when able to use free associations. We have to impose limitations; the analyst could not work if the analysand were free to resort to physical violence. When a patient comes with firearms the analyst has to rely on physical alertness to deal with such a potentially dangerous situation. It is less serious when the patient substitutes a musical instrument for the gun—although some types of musical instrument can make the analyst's interpretations inaudible. One instrument that is usually available is the ability to scream. I have mentioned elsewhere the trained singer who is able to scream in a way not open to less gifted or less well trained people, and who can thereby make an analytic session painful for the analyst.

What are we to think about the patient who does not want to lie on the couch? Is it possible that lying on a couch subjects them to physical pressures of a kind which are beyond their capacity to tolerate, or to verbalize, or to 'understand'? The analyst cannot interpret the 'sights' a fetus could 'see' if subjected to pressure on the optic pits. This is an object of research by the analyst in the course of a psycho-analysis where he has the opportunity for detailed and prolonged contact with patients. If he can also discuss differing experiences with different observers there is hope of seeing what is observed in common. It is one of the justifications for an analytic society.

There are difficulties analogous to those associated with the caesura of birth. A similar caesura seems to exist between the inhabitant, say, of the East and of the West. Some of these similarities/differences are spectacular, particularly in time; the mystics express themselves in terms which are strikingly similar although sometimes separated from each other by many hundreds of years. How is one to penetrate this obstacle, this caesura of birth? Can any method of communication be sufficiently 'penetrating' to pass that caesura in the direction from post-natal conscious thought back to the pre-mental in which thoughts and ideas have their counterpart in 'times' or 'levels' of mind where they are not thoughts or ideas? That penetration has to be effective in either direction. It is easy to put it in pictorial terms by saying it is like penetrating into the woman's inside either from inside out, as at birth, or from outside in, as in sexual intercourse. These pictorial formulations are primitive and general; they may be so general that it is difficult to see what is to be said at any precise moment—which is the analyst's problem. One cannot go back—although we talk about it in those words—to childhood or infancy. It is in the present that we have to have a method of formulation which can penetrate the barrier.

If, as I think, our constant problem is that of choice, this also involves inhibition. Thus, if I want to give one interpretation I have to inhibit other interpretations which I am *not* choosing to give. This is usually fairly simple because the choice is between a number of consciously entertained ideas; it is not easy when the inhibition has a pathological quality which makes it more difficult to entertain an unwelcome idea. Choice involves what some of us call 'splitting'; perhaps four or five possible interpretations must be considered. The human personality exists as a whole; we have to split that personality to formulate several possible ideas or interpretations. That I call non-pathological splitting. We have to find some method by which those particular interpretations can be put into an order before establishing which one is to be given precedence. This has to be done in a way which is not the same as talking about it—'doing' must be quicker. The interpretation has to be made at the right moment; it is, therefore, necessary that this non-pathological splitting, ordering of those splits and choice of formulation become part of a rapid and practised mind.

The analyst is restricted to what is available to him from his experience of his own life on the one hand, and to what he considers to be the facts which are unfolding in his presence on the other. In the practice of psycho-analysis the analyst has the advantage of the presence of the analysand. The possibilities are open-ended; we do not know what the analysand is likely to say or do to express himself and his character. The analyst is dependent on such facts as are made available to him while the patient is present and available for observation. What the patient does away from the session cannot be known to the analyst; hearsay evidence is fallacious and of small value in comparison with the direct evidence.

An infant can show a startled reaction to certain forms of stimulus. On the other hand there are stimuli which are consciously more striking to us as adults, but which pass the infant by. In an obstetric ward a baby will show no signs of awareness of the slamming of a door although it is obtrusive to the adult observer. In analysis the analyst likewise has an opportunity of observing certain reactions which are 'slight' but may, nevertheless, be of significance and therefore worth while bringing to the patient's attention. These trivial movements or noises show up clearly with the patient who is virtually inarticulate or silent, in contrast with the prevailing silence. This kind of experience is difficult to convey to a non-participant; it is one of the problems of communication with colleagues who, however experienced in analysis, cannot be familiar with the experience that the analyst has with a *particular* analysand. No terms—'autistic child', 'psychotic', 'borderline'—are of much use because the experience in an analysis is more subtle, detailed and difficult to divide up into these somewhat crude divisions available to us when we borrow from the practice of medicine, or existing philosophies, or analytic theories.

Since analysis takes place in time, the tendency is to believe that when the patient is talking he is describing a state of affairs that is also 'ordered' in time; patient and analyst are liable to think of something as having happened in the past. This obscures the fact that we exist in the *present*; we can do nothing about the past. It is, therefore, seriously misleading to think as if we dealt with the past. What makes the venture of analysis difficult is that one constantly changing personality talks to another. But the personality does not seem to develop as it would if it were a piece of elastic being stretched out. It is as if it were something which developed many different skins as an onion does. This point adds importance to the factor of the caesura, the need to penetrate what is recognized as a dramatic event like birth, or a possibility of success, or a breakdown. The patient has a breakup, or breakdown, rather than a 'breakthrough'. Many a façade has been saved by the misfortune that has made it a successful ruin.

I do not wish to abandon the idea of the conscious or unconscious; the existing theories are valuable, when properly used, either for thinking about a situation or for illuminating the situation for the sake of someone not-self. These ideas that we hear in the course of analysis have at some time been interpretations though now free associations. We are dealing with a series of skins which have been epidermis or conscious, but are now 'free associations'.

The ability of the analysand to take advantage of the possibility of success which has opened out is a symptom of the penetration from the situation which Freud describes as intra-uterine, to the situation which is conscious and post-caesural. I do not suggest that the event is related to the dramatic episode of birth itself, but rather that that dramatic situation, if borne in mind, is easier to use as a model to understand far less dramatic occasions which occur over and over again when the patient is challenged to move from one state of mind to another. In other words, to penetrate an obstacle or layer between the states when opportunity opens out, or there is some apparently disastrous state of affairs to be turned to good account. Since we can do nothing about the dramatic or obvious external event, it provides an interpretation, later to become a free association, for the not-at-all-obvious event.

I want now to consider a non-analytic situation, namely that in which the patient has to deal with changes in his affairs by making decisions. This situation is comparable with the game of Snakes and Ladders. The patient's choice may fall on the head of a snake and he returns to an apparently unfortunate state of affairs which he deplores and regrets; or he may arrive at a ladder and find himself in the position of being able to make several moves which are towards his final goal—which he may also regret. In either situation the choice that the patient makes compels readjustment to the consequences. Much then depends on the extent to which he is a victim of self-hatred or self-love.

The situation of the analyst is similar to that of the analysand in that he lives in a world of reality of which the analysis itself is a part. He therefore has to make choices, including the possibility of having to keep silent because he does not know an answer or cannot think of an appropriate interpretation; he can indulge himself by giving an interpretation which is only a way of passing the time.

Consider a decision which confronts most people—whether to propose marriage or to accept a proposal. Either way the two people have to make a decision. I quote from Yeats's poem on this precise dilemma, 'Solomon and the Witch':

For though love has a spider's eye
To find out some appropriate pain—
Aye, though all passion's in the glance—
For every nerve, and tests a lover
With cruelties of Choice and Chance;
And when at last that murder's over
Maybe the bride-bed brings despair,
For each an imagined image brings
And finds a real image there;

Like birth, the caesura of marriage is dramatic; it may obscure the fact that the events at the time of marriage and after are influenced by events which take place long before the marriage. As Freud put it with regard to birth, events in the patient's mind are greatly influenced by events which were in fact intra-uterine. Using this for theoretical purposes, events which are in the womb of time eventually show themselves in the conscious life of the person concerned who then has to act in the situation which has now become actual.

There are any number of different caesuras. How are they to be traversed? We must reconsider the transitive characteristic of the free association and the interpretation. Opposed to that there is what we might call the situation at which the patient or the analyst wishes ultimately to arrive—the 100 mark on the Snakes and Ladders board. There are plenty of snakes and ladders on the way during the course of the transition from one to the other. Each free association and each interpretation represents the change in the situation which we psycho-analyse. Even the wrong interpretation causes change; misinformation in the form of false—deliberately false—statements changes the situation. How quickly can we become aware of the changed situation, and how quickly can we see what good use could be made of that changed situation even though adverse?

The likelihood of meeting old friends there makes the prospect of Hell less frightening than the prospect of Heaven for which life on earth has given no adequate preparation.

But this also applies to decisions which are made over and again. One may deplore an unfortunate decision; how terrible it might be if we never made unfortunate decisions or unfortunate interpretations. In analysis it is recovery from the unfortunate decision, the use of the mistaken decision that we have to accustom overselves to deal with. In this view of the position there is no question of a cure.

It has been said that the English and Americans have everything in common except the language. The same could be said of the analyst and the analysand; the language is apparently the one existing means of communication. Nevertheless it is also the one thing which they do not appear to have in common probably because they are talking from different vertices. A mountain viewed from different points of the compass *may* be recognizably the same mountain, but it may be such a different view that it appears to be an entirely different mountain. Consider the patient who says that he is seriously troubled by blushing, but to the view of the analyst appears to be almost invariably marked by an extreme pallor. Is it possible that the patient who rejects blushing does so by inhibiting his blood flow in such a way that he does anything but blush—the place of the blush is taken by this great pallor? I do not suggest that this is actually the case, but I think it is useful to be able to air these 'hunches' as a transitive statement on the way to an interpretation. It is important to get used to this transitive method of thinking with a view to arriving at an interpretation, which is also arriving at an immediately changing situation; whether the interpretation is correct or incorrect, fresh interpretations will have to be made in order to meet that changed situation.

Suppose the patient does not want to lie on the couch and, having taken his place on a chair, then displays considerable restlessness and has to change to a different chair. This may be the reaction to sensations generated in the autonomic system, or from the stimulation by the CNS (in turn generated by the unpleasing sight of chair or couch). It could account for dreams of which the patient can give no account, or of which he gives a narrative account with no free associations. They would be inappropriate if he has had not what we would ordinarily call a dream, but a sense of muscular position which has reflected itself in his having a sleepless night.

Having had a dream which is in fact a sensuous experience, the patient then has to find a dream which is more in conformity with what he thinks is expected of him by the analyst. He will often betray the fact that it is not an ordinary dream by the absence of free associations. This applies particularly to a patient who is afraid that he is psychotic, or that he is going mad. He prefers to behave and speak in a way which he regards as neurotic and less severe than a psychosis. Conversely, the patient makes statements to which he attaches little importance and which he hopes the analyst may regard as unimportant; for example, the patient who complained of blushing. Some patients repeatedly state that they have some particular experience and then give the reason why—making it part and parcel of their formulation. This continued repetition suggests a state of mind which is proper to a person who only lives in a causal world. But the only world in which causes can be said to be a prominent feature is the world of *things*—not the world of people, or characters, or personalities. The patient who is always telling us that he feels such-and-such 'because . . .', is avoiding a particular relationship which exists between one character and another.

We need to re-view commonplace formulations—psychotic, neurotic, psycho-somatic, soma-psychotic and so forth—to consider, from our own experience, what we think those things are when we meet them. A patient may complain about headaches together with a number of plausible explanations which are probably correct. *Rational* interpretations might be adequate if they were the only important ones, but what may appeal to the human mind because it seems to be logical, or to fit in with such powers of logic as we have, may be by no means the correct interpretation of the factual situation which is beyond our comprehension or experience. To distort that experience in order to make it fit into such capacities as we have is a dangerous thing. On the other hand it is equally dangerous for an analyst to think that medicine, art, religion are inadequate to describe or make it possible for us to be consciously aware of the actual phenomena of reality. The analyst has to use what we hope is a non-pathological method of splitting because the total situation that presents itself to us is beyond our capacity, just as we suppose that it is beyond the capacity of the infant to have a grasp of the world as we know it as adults. It is natural for the infant to see a *part* of the world of reality; that particular view is not wrong—it is inadequate. To limit ourselves to the observation only of what we understand is denying ourselves the raw material on which present and possibly future wisdom and knowledge might depend. The fact that it is incomprehensible now, because our minds are unsuitable or ill-fitted to grasp it, is not a reason for limiting the facts such as are actually available.

It is possible that the splits in which we have to indulge as analysts, as adults, make it possible to see some things which the patient, or child, or infant can see and vice versa; they are essential to discrimination. This could be said to be one of the advantages of marriage; the two partners can, as it were, pool their defects and thereby also pool their wisdom. In analysis we are seeing a total personality who has at some time, consciously or unconsciously, chosen a particular view or a particular vertex from which to see the view. This always involves inhibition of the capacity to see the views that one does not want to see. The psychotic patient may be anxious to suppress, be blind to or unaware of what the sane person is able to see; the character is psychosis minus neurosis, or psychosis minus sanity, or sanity (rationality) minus neurosis or minus psychosis. The important thing is not that a patient is a borderline psychotic, or a psychotic, or a neurotic, but that he is a total character *minus* . . . and then we have to form our own judgment of what that patient is minus, whether the person who is almost a caricature of robust commonsense and sanity is not really a character who lacks important components because he believes that a psychotic is 'mad' or 'insane', or that someone would think him insane if it were known that he had such thoughts or ideas. We could regard artists, musicians, scientists, discoverers as those who have dared to entertain these transitive thoughts and ideas. It is in course of transit, in the course of changing from one position to another, that these people seem to be most vulnerable—as, for example, during adolescence or latency. At the same time they are vulnerable to the observation of others who cannot tolerate the totality of the human personality, and therefore cannot tolerate someone who is so 'mad', so 'curious', so 'eccentric', or so 'sane'. I remember a fellow officer in the army complaining of 'the robust commonsense' of another officer. He said, 'That man makes me understand why people talk about "rude health"; I have never known a person who seemed to be so rude as he does by being so healthy'. Making due allowance for the jealousy and envy which is directed towards what a person is able to be, there is nevertheless something to be said for noticing the hostility and resistance which is stirred up by the creature which is different from ourselves, or the state of mind which is different from our own, or our own state of mind which is so different from that which we like to think we can always present to our fellows.

Thus we have returned to this problem of how to transcend the caesura when one is in movement from one state of mind to another; how to surpass the various obstacles in the course of a psychological or spiritual journey of development; whether to regard those obstacles as pathological, needing pathological terms to describe them, or whether they are in fact non-pathological. In the psycho-analytic experience we are concerned both with the translation in the direction of what we do not know into something which we do know or which we can communicate, and also from what we do know and can communicate to what we do not know and are not aware of because it is unconscious and which may even be pre-natal, or pre-birth of a psyche or a mental life, but is part of a physical life in which at some stage a physical impulse is immediately translated into a physical action. That transitive experience from a passive to an active physical state may reflect itself even when we are dealing with potentially rational and articulate persons. Can we detect in these expressions of conscious rational communications vestiges of something coming from a part of the personality which is in fact physical? Sometimes we call it psycho-somatic medicine; at other times it does not even become sufficiently obvious in the mental life of the patient for us to be able to detect that it is arising from an area of a person *in the present*, although it might once have existed simply primitively and in the realm of physical action. This involves taking a different view about the obstacles to psycho-analytic progress, the development of the relationship between analyst and analysand, and considering phenomena which present themselves in the actual analytic situation, but which have not usually been interpreted—may never have been interpreted even by the patient—into terms which are communicable in the realms of articulate speech or articulate thought. I do not suggest that we can interpret something like a migrainous headache in psychological terms. This is one of the difficulties about the sort of communication which is possible in lectures, supervisions, discussions between colleagues; a supposition or hunch or suspicion, such as I make when I suggest the possibility that the fortification of light patterns which present themselves to certain types of headache really come from pre-natal levels of mind, may seem to be offering an easy explanation of something which is extremely complex, thereby interfering with, and itself becoming an obstacle to, psycho-analytic research in the one situation in which it can really be carried out—in the consulting room with such patients as present themselves for analysis. What I am putting forward as a mere suspicion or conjecture may be turned into a theory, or treated as if it were something which could be used for immediate translation into an interpretation. In so far as that is possible what I say becomes more of a liability than an asset. An analyst reading this paper must be able to forget it, to dismiss it from his mind, unless something is said by the analysand which calls it into his consciousness and causes him then to formulate it in such language as he is able to use.

Has this discussion any *practical* value for a psycho-analyst? It is a question which I fear may be provoked by my stress on practice rather than theory, not only theory of psycho-analysis but of anything—finance, political science, mathematics, painting, music and so on. The only material I have to study is a human character that can study me also and is free to walk out of my office if and when it chooses. As I cannot—within the bounds of civility and respect for facts—I must find some way of engaging the person in conversation of a kind that he might be able to tolerate while material presents itself for my assessment. A painter could estimate the quality of the canvas on which to practise his art; a sculptor might discern the grain of the wood or marble which he contemplates; the composer might allow his 'inner' eye to be impinged upon the sight, or his 'inner' ear upon the sounds, from which he chooses to discriminate and then transforms into music. How is the psycho-analyst to transform his assessment of the person who comes to see him professionally? Into a learned article? An interpretation? A printed judgment?

Suppose the analysand begins, to all appearance, to weep. The analyst becomes aware of his own funds of compassion and is impelled to participate with caution lest his responses, like a chisel of tempered steel cutting into balsa wood, too easily fashion a pattern of which the effect could not be obliterated or corrected. The analyst is affected by the patient's tears which may trace out channels in his composure no less lasting than the excoriations which he has feared to produce in his patient. He must, therefore, be sensitive to the difference in real life—not in theory—between 'tears', and 'moisture' extruded from the bodily surface open to his inspection, both his own and the analysand's.

Rephrasing Freud's statement for my own convenience: There is much more continuity between autonomically appropriate quanta and the waves of conscious thought and feeling than the impressive caesura of transference and counter-transference would have us believe. So . . .? Investigate the caesura; not the analyst; not the analysand; not the unconscious; not the conscious; not sanity; not insanity. But the caesura, the link, the synapse, the (counter-trans)-ference, the transitive-intransitive mood.

At this point I cannot proceed for lack of the very elements which have not yet been discovered or elaborated. It is typical of decision which has to serve the human at those junctures when knowledge is not there to be used.